YOU

For Afiniki Kyari

YOU

JOHN HAYNES

SEREN

Seren is the book imprint of
Poetry Wales Press Ltd.
57 Nolton Street, Bridgend, Wales, CF31 3AE
www.serenbooks.com

ISBN: 978-1-85411-517-1

A CIP record for this title is available from the British Library.

The publisher acknowledges the financial assistance of the Welsh Books Council.

Printed in Bembo by Bell & Bain, Glasgow

Author's website/blog:jhaynestab.co.uk

When we consider a case like Dante's we are powerfully reminded of the reasons which have supported a view of love quite contrary to that advocated by evolutionary psychology. Love, it is suggested, is a cultural construct; and the way it is constructed depends upon various features of a given society. For example, in a society such as ours in which adults very often live alone until they fall in love, love is closely connected to overcoming loneliness. But this could hardly be a major feature of the experience of life in a society in which – until marriage – the individual would normally live in the closest proximity to an extended family.

    – John Armstrong: *Conditions of love: the philosophy of intimacy*

The first and second persons *I* and *you* naturally retain this deictic sense; their meaning is defined in the act of speaking.

    – M. A. K. Halliday: *Functional Grammar*

Mirror neurons may well be the key to our ability to understand the emotional state of mind of another person....

    – Robert Winston: *Human Instinct*

I don't know when I'll ever see her,
Our countries are so far apart.
Yes, there are roads enough between them,
but it's not roads that separate us.

    – Jaufre Rudel (after Bernard O'Donohue's prose translation in his
    The Courtly Love Tradition)

And there's the ECWA school and that's Miss Bosse
turning at her wall map of the ancient
trade routes that the Buzus used to cross,
all that blank sand she tries with so much passion
in her English to make real beyond
the blowing door-cloth and the lizard sprawled
out flat and still and listening on the wall

as if its nodding birthmark-indigo
and orange head nodded in empathy
with her, with you, your letters traced into
a tray of sand, your hush in Jesus' holy
name, your walk back home on paths through guinea
corn, the floating pile of textbooks balanced
on your head with all the nonchalance

that comes of something learnt and then forgotten
that it has been, like the history
of who the person is lost in the person
bearing it, then in the words somebody
tells the tale in, then the mimicry
inside the nerves of that, its whispers to
some inner, mouthed, imaginary *you*,

ECWA: Evangelical Church of West Africa
Buzus: used in colloquial Hausa for Tuareg traditionally involved in
the trans-Saharan trade before the European presence in West Africa.

who's coming still towards me through the sky,
seat-back and plaits reflected in the cabin
glass, the wing stretched over bevelled sea,
although the plane's not there at all, has been
recalled long since, in fact, because of some
ground to air threat out of Algiers. And so
my empathy is wrong. It isn't you.

You come alone – National Express to Southsea
South Parade, the street, the bed-sit, Jack
that creepy landlord ringing Dad to okay
forcing up the window, and I'm back
to find my gas-fire on, the mattress dragged
up close to it, and among shaking huge
wild table-leg and chair-back shadows: you

swathed in my coat and woollen hat under
the duvet, and already gone back home
as people do so far asleep – Kagoma
or our house in Zaria, the dream
wasp fizzingly inside a mango skin
as loud as is this gas fire coming through
the skin and sleep of *was* and *here* and *you* –

but not quite me, not yet perhaps, this someone
watching till your eyelids come awake
with his gaze on them and again you come
into the ancient mirroring he makes
you, mimes you, in, a kind of second sight
or so I think of it, held in the eyes
that look back from the gaze inside the gaze

of someone loved because they happened, *are* –
the little tadpole, its moon tide, the blue
green dew that gently falleth on the grass,
the see-through lub and dub that we see through
the scan, and shape our lips into some *you*
that can be made to stand for anyone
who's ever lived, but stands for you alone,

held in the isolating flesh. I want
to think of love, to learn to think of it,
as an attempt and nothing more, and fond
indeed at that, as if the trickster spirit
in his mime mimes just this genesis,
and just in that, perhaps, beyond the prose
of space and edge some circle does get closed.

You've come so very far because of me.
A dream, I'm looking for you in a dream.
And there's the Sabo market and Dan Ladi's
splayed toes on the *Birmingham* worked in
the treadle of his sewing machine. The rim
of its brass wheel as it whirs balances
a spark of sunlight and it's motionless –

half something out of Jung, half this forgotten
slave trade iron and thread filling his stare.
A line of sweat runs through itself down from
his temple as the needle guns and hair
shows in the armhole of his shirt, half stranger
to the family as he's always been –
who meets my half-brother-in-law half-grin

half way, stranger to stranger, he whose scissors
slice the cotton through, whose stitches hum
and click exact, exact, who needs no inches
no, nor tape measure, who now I've come
will look at me, and sew dis so-so hem
for hand, for neck, dis so-so leg, who knows
just by his eye just how I fit my clothes.

Sabo: short for *Sabon Gari*, strangers' area in a northern Nigerian city
dis so-so: this kind of, one like this

So he's my guide? Now there's a farm, then ridges,
then we're cutting down the two-men-tall
stalks of the guinea corn. Then there are kids
lowering Dulux cans into a well
on lengths of waste industrial rubber. Pestles
echo through the dusk. A frog hangs from
the surface tension by its gaze alone.

And now mud walls on which the lizards cling,
and candles, raffia mats, and I'm the stranger
welcomed and welcomed. Somebody's singing –
you – and your dead father's standing there.
And as you sing, the deeds he did, however
ordinary once, make his eyes wet
with joy. He shakes and shakes and shakes his head.

I've read about The Ancestors, those who
long since have turned to soil and yet can whisper
still, like him in not-quite speech, so you
yourself have to pronounce the words. So far
he's come, like you, this spirit on our sofa,
Malam Kyari self watching TV
in his embroidered cap and kaftani.

Kaftani: Kaftan

There was a discipline: first cockerel
get firewood, sweep the compound, carry water
from the stream, the three hours' trek to school,
then back, then cook, then prayers, Mamma and Babba
always one about the rules. "My daughters,
my sons..." He called you all before he died,
and spoke of the abstractions truth and pride.

You worked hard, certain, always, that the shadow
of his head would fall, sooner or later,
on your exercise book, wait there, no
movement or word, maybe the raffia
just clicking as he left, his feet as ever
soundless. Then he died. You were eleven.
There'd been no point in all the homework, then.

Each evening, now, back from the hospital,
you tell me how it went and what you did –
like those times when you'd come home from your school,
and telling through the day to him, then, made
its time turn real. It may be as you've said,
he'd never have accepted me, but still
his spirit's welcome here. He makes us real.

And you there in that hollow hall (a pupil
should be loved thought Socrates), the dress
with polka dots on it among the little
tables set in rows to take your test
in someone else's English, someone else's
electronic hands to circle through
those six right angles allocated you

as time allowed to write the sentences
and pass, and get away, not from that ghost
always behind your chair, but someone else
his house, his chores, his rules, his little jokes
about your lower lip, about your specs:
the portrait that he drew on that cave wall
inside your skull makes faces at you still.

Now when I kiss your neck you study on
without a word. To get the care plan right,
the dosage, the blood-count: this is for no-one
else: desk, books, silence, angle-poise light.
Exile again. Sometimes your eyes will slide
away from mine as if this isn't home,
or if it is, you're the more here alone.

In a strange land you sing the harmonies
to Hausa hymns, the same ones you sang then –
your agile alto line, or else Bob Marley
or the Babylon of Boney M –
in that house everyone called Number 10,
the squork and squark of bull frogs in the pond,
which, if I listen hard, still turns to song.

Better than me, you know the mums at school,
recycling days, the music scene, the times
of soaps, and people find you *jovial*,
your word, unerringly *Nigerian*,
you with that shine of friendliness behind
your specs, and here and this is to be home
because here is the sun where *I* was born.

Yet who you are is not quite here, is called
from somewhere else with orange earth between
your toes splayed like a bush-woman's for all
the Clarks you walk the supermarkets in.
I close my eyes and float through Number Ten:
a wrapper lying on the bed, a faint
coo-croo up in the roof, your wet footprints.

the sun where I was born: Desdemona's words – "...I think the sun/where he
was born/Drew all such humours from him"

And then the day we turned into the bush
and followed just the lines of other tyres
with grass between them so you felt its hush
against the bumper, or a squeal of briars,
and jolts that rocked our thighs about. Then Kwoi,
the ancient village with its history
of people's voices bearing memories,

and your gran's compound, that boy very still
outside her room holding a cup of water
with both hands. We waited also till,
not sure she'd woken up, he called out "Kakka"
very softly just in case, then, when her
voice creaked from the dark, went in, his feet
scuff-shuffling the dust so's not to spill it.

Roof-thatch, brushed clay floor, clay bed, a wrapper
over her. She spoke from where she lay.
"Few days, one week, you no go see me, shah."
She drank, then smiled. She wasn't scared. She'd see
them all again, parents, sisters. "Bature,
you are welcome. How are you? Sannu!"
I answered: "Na gode". It means "Thank you."

Kakka: grandma
few days: in a few days' time
shah: I assure you (informal)
Bature: European, Whiteman
Sannu: hello

What for? The confidence? Although I had
no sort of faith like that, just in the moment
that she spoke I saw them reaching glad
arms round each other, ululations, brilliant
cloths new from the market, newly ironed,
the creases making little silver blades
that broke and bent and flashed from daze to shade

and back, such happiness as wouldn't ever
come again, there couldn't ever be
a second gratitude like this, such utter
staring disbelief, that suddenly
pushed in between my thoughts in spite of me,
or no: in spite of them, is it? – like one
of those reptile brain spirits out of Jung?

Then sunlight, rainbow lizards scattering
across the wall, and no trace in their genes –
or is it hope? – of any empathy
to come, inside a sinking mist of grains
of sand, no suckling lips or tongue, or gaze
that mirrors back the mirror paradise
held safe there for a moment in her eyes.

In England God was different, though, the words
of prayers all written down, the people's cheeks
set flat and serious, and afterwards
a bare room with a hatch for cups of tea
where they relax at last and yet still speak
with tensely friendly smiles. Hello, I'm Jack
or Joan and haven't noticed that you're black.

I thought about that wedding in Kaduna
with the keyboard and guitars and drums,
how from their empty mouths the alleluias
lifted, and they held their upturned palms
before them, waiting, and when Jesus comes
Elli contorts her mouth, and wrings her hands
and stares hard through the air in which he stands.

Then Pastor Joshua: *marriage is lent
to us, is lent, not to the couple only,
not them only: Jesus too is present…*
then I saw this profile next to me
outlined in silver on the pillow slowly
blinking in the dark. The son of man.
Someone made strange just by his human form,

the form we leave behind ourselves to change
into the lovers on the screen, *alone*
together as they are, and touch and merge
and grow imaginary, and we've become –
what, genii, is it? – see-through among
mirrors and chairs, close as our history
of them, which is too close to touch, maybe.

Like forms of speaking, coloured glass, stone, paint,
that made a distant world inside the skull,
and trekked the dark places of it, his face
sometimes an African's, his truths made truthful
differently. There on your classroom wall
he hung, part tortured terrorist, part stern
Victorian clergyman, part ancestor.

What would a chat with Jesus Christ be like?
Getting to know him, trying not to strain
to *be myself*, there in that room, that dark
where you'd first slept with me and where you came
rushing with joy to say *I'm born again*,
a week, was it, a few days maybe, after
that, your eyes made wet with cosmic laughter?

I thought of Dad and that *Tales from the Bible*
that he read me, bedtime, curtains parted,
outside all the fences of the council
estate gardens spread out in a star
of steel wire spokes, and Mr Reece next door,
clinking his spade as in that dressing gown,
the Lord trod ripples like an eiderdown.

God's voice, Dad made deep down and scary. Jesus
though, was quiet, the accompanier
who even so was hardly someone else
at all, not even at that prep school where
I walked the woods and blubbed. They were as near
to me, the words that Jesus spoke, as Dad's
chin and the smell of that hair oil he had.

Which never brought his hair back, as it didn't
Shaka's either, or, rather the flecks
of grey that vanished in the Whiteman's potion
didn't take old age with them. "Expect
he thought that next," our History master quipped,
"he'd walk on water!" as, once in that school,
I dreamt he did, across the swimming pool.

The racism remains, and just as puerile.
Someone yells a question at your car
as you get in, and you can turn, sick smile
into his shaking pupils, shift the gear,
and drive off with, or so it feels, just anger
as the shops and signs steady towards
you from a past long since already yours...

old Don, for instance, who would groan and curse
in whispers when you had to wash his groin,
and Meg who held both of your hands in hers
to watch the World Cup on the television,
crying, saying thank you, thank you, then
when you got in next day you found the mattress
stripped: a watch, a ring, a crucifix.

A job that you could get, new in UK:
indignity and helplessness to wipe
away, and faces suddenly awake
and scared and shouting in the night,
no loved-ones left with time for them, these white
old people who had learnt to call your name.
You came with your black hands and washed them clean.

And at the hospital our neighbour's daughter
in the lift who when you smiled smiled back
at you as if towards a friendly stranger,
since the shadow and the shine and black
across your brow and eyes and nose and cheeks
met nothing in that history she had
for keeping shapes of faces in her head

although she'd met you only days before,
or you'd met her, stretching your arm across
the hedge to shake, but that was somewhere else,
and now, back in the ward, the teenie nurses,
who twist mouths and eyes around because
you know more words than they do in their English,
smile without the flicker of a lash

far off indeed, and later, you can rest
and thumb slap through the catalogue you've got
to find a mobile phone for me, the best
deal and how long to pay and how much off,
under the perfumed foam of some car wash
which as we listen to your latest Keane
hisses as fiercely as Kagoma rain.

Respect for somebody because they've been
alive so long, their breasts are used, they heal
the sick, they teach.... *The people here, they seem –*
I know that customs aren't the same – but people
here. At home no child would dare to scramble
like that past an old man getting on
a bus and not a word from anyone.

It's not... and yes, what comes into the head
is Grandma's word, Miss Bosse's word as well:
not *civilized*, Victorian indeed,
like a baturiya telling the tale
that Jesus told about the word for soul
translated into earth, rock, birds, wind, weeds,
your father trudging through a cloud of seeds.

And here's the Green Man that your son's Year Three
have made for parents' evening, candle soul
through cutout eyes, dreadlocks that were spaghetti
once, his smock of lettuce leaves, a whole
red pepper of a heart, (*But how can people*
make statues of food!) and roots of ginger
for his naked clumps of feet. A leper's.

baturiya: (Hausa) European woman. Etymology uncertain,
but possibly from 'Victoria'

No aunts, grandmas, cousins, those second mothers
in a compound. Us alone to rock
and soothe away the cosmic baby terrors
for him with the melody of talk
that means nothing, means *love*, until he stopped,
and we could hear the birds. You are the only
Africa your son has got. Plus me.

And I'm already old. I called him Tristan,
therefore, he who's growing now to love
me – is that possible? – too much, the one
soonest to slide into the laps and hugs
that make his home. *Dad, look! Dad, look!* – You shrug
and smile how it's me in particular
he shows the moon in his binoculars.

A child is like a soul. That outlives us.
That starts off wholly physical and then
is slowly transmigrating as it must,
a voice, a face, a bike left on the lawn,
because love's also made of metaphors
of other things. We become sentences.
We get translated into something else.

Dad, what's it like to die? And when you're dead
will you still hear me play the violin?
Will you be you? Or just the word instead
of you? No, I'll be *you*. I'll snuggle in
your memory like hide and seek again.
The similes he knows are not quite lies
are not quite tears, quite standing in his eyes.

We watch The Four Seasons played by a fifteen
year old girl. First there are daffodils
behind her, and her cotton dress is green,
changing to blue on blue sky with a circle
of white sun, high up and small, then whirling
dead leaves on a stream, the dress auburn,
then frost on glass like silver fronds of fern.

The bow creaks slowly up, swoops juddering,
then plucks and plinks the drips. The time will come
for both of us when it's embarrassing
for him to lie his cheek like this along
my chest, rubbing my jumper with his thumb,
since love is not, whatever kind we mean,
like daffodils, each spring the same again.

Or other seasons, like those of the Buzu
family we met as we drove back,
as into sky after that first night? – *Blue
People*, so far from home, so tightly packed
there on their camel between hump and neck,
the black robed man, the wife, the child, its springy
lope, their leather bags and bare feet swinging,

so far inland from the desert – home
which didn't seem like home, not in the way
I'd think of that, as somewhere closely known,
and fixed, owned and owning, a sense of place
not theirs, which is to do with kinds of space
of sky, of rock, or thorn, or grains of sand
so fine they turn to air and then to mind –

or I imagined, through the windscreen glass
as they came on until the tufts of fur
and folds of knee skin loomed and then were past,
but not, of course, just like the poem Wordsworth
wrote, the one on memory you'd learnt
at school, not knowing what they were, until
I told you, those creatures called *daffodils*...

Buzu (Hausa): Tuareg's servant, or as here (colloquially) Tuareg,
also known as 'Blue People'.

as real outside our English kitchen window
as the yam you turn in groundnut oil
and dip the suya pieces in borkono,
thread them onto skewers, close the grill:
exotic daffs, the common asphodels
each common soul finds on that desert plain
where thoughts turn into plumes of breath and then

to air, and so this is amnesia
not memory at all, is it? – the loss
of who he was, in Dorothy's own here
and now, her boat, her lake, her lonely grass,
of what his eyes, in hers, could see because
loss is precise, and fixed, as if fixed there
defiantly behind his long dead stare.

His *Narcissus botanica*, that lost
myth whose gaze now is just the gazed-at light
on pools whose surfaces are just his past
in him, his yen to love himself going right
through to the flower as such, the child inside
the man: himself, *ourselves*, which in your father's
other English would have meant: *each other.*

suya (Hausa): Kebab
borkono: a kind of pepper.
asphodel: from which the word 'daffodil' is derived.
They grow in the 'Fields of Asphodel', the place not
of memory, but of forgetfulness

Dad planted them. They come back every April
round the Cox's orange pippin roots,
the time for love or so my medieval
folklore had it once, the rustic flutes
carved out of hedgerow sticks, as if the notes
had lifted through the sap, as if the beat
of drums came through the mud into our feet –

now more like childhood, and those sand martins
shrieking around me as I climbed to steal
the eggs from nests down arm deep burrows in
the sandstone, just some – proto sexual,
it seems now – need to reach right in and feel
the white straw and the down, and didn't know
they'd crossed the desert, sleeping as they flew,

for that small fawn and white shell that I stored
gently inside my mouth as I climbed down
again and pricked each end once with a thorn,
then gently blew, then watched the stuff come out
like shaking phlegm, caught in the wind, that loot
from Africa in cotton wool to keep
beside my bed as weightlessly as sleep;

that they flew back across the whole Sahara
sleeping on the wing, as you begin
to now, with those small sounds, back to Kagoma –
that house where I met your mother in
her starched tall headtie and her Dutch wax print
and just a little shy to meet your White
Man, but so glad with wrinkles smiling tight –

just as I bend across you, turn the lamp
off, draw the curtains, thinking with what skill
I managed it on that rickety camp
bed, making love with not the faintest squeal
or crunk of springs. Like press-ups, I recall,
rugby-fit then, mouth open while I howled
into the dark not letting out a sound,

or that night, at the dam, when we made love,
remember, there beside the road, half in
the car half out, with confidence enough
to dare the world to drive towards us, then,
with full light on, and nights at Number Ten,
insane with flesh, and resurrected new
again each time as neither I nor you.

And Lara born almost the day your mother
died, a second soul, the joy and sorrow
child across all this school map Sahara,
tongues, customs, the slow notes of a cello
from her room that stops us in the hall
to listen to her shape the melody,
of that mute swan she's lost in totally

as I am, staring stupid out across
the parked cars and the house fronts she, your Mum,
could never... me thinking again of loss
of who somebody is, the I am sum
and end beyond which, well the others come
and in their heads it's *I* as much, and true,
as I've also ever been *I* or *you*,

and then the door-bell rings, and she comes out
surprised we're standing here and wonders why
we haven't gone for it, pauses, then "What?"
then "What? What?" as if there's something we
are hiding, weird as we are, totally
unlike in every thing, she says, "you two,"
still grinning, "you, you two, the two of you."

Of yous? Of years, of shapes of rooms, of towns,
of death and then a tag around a baby's
wrist, of what they kept from you, since how –
since what – could you... so very far away,
and next day phone trolley – Comfort, Elli:
go later, too late, and ethereal
sun on the grass of West Brom General,

barges, canals, Paul Robeson singing on
the tape recorder as she went to sleep
with my arms round her, yet so much – how? – gone
for all that joy, things now I still can't keep
straight in my head, as narrative, a shape
which wasn't one, or I can't make it so –
you crazy pair, the two of you, you two –

each looking at a different street outside,
through different panes, and yes sometimes there seems
nothing but village bluntness in the eyes
set in your specs, an anger at the rooms
themselves with no-one there, no-one, no mum,
no sisters, no children who'll run and fetch,
and that man at some writing at some desk,

who'll be your astronaut, though, who'll be weightless
won't he, lifting until high turns to deep
and he'll come back at breakfast time and, yes,
be *I*, smiling as if there's been no bleep
or lub that mission control couldn't keep
in contact with: just suddenly with cheers
hugs, leapings behind monitors, he's there –

the famous orbiter of orbiting,
sticking it out, keeping that inner face
calm as a watermark, for having trust in
having trust that it's your tilting cosmos
in the screens he watches, and he knows
like wings, like home, curled in that egg-smooth cell
with planets shaking on its single wall,

your whole Earth with its curves of indigo,
its smears of white, its lizard-scale-like mountains,
its Great Wall, its Afrikas and Inds
without which he... these Ithacas, these souths
and norths, these shirts and dresses screaming round
inside the porthole – or at dusk, a small
lamp on the lawn lit by a solar cell.

Love doesn't have to be returned, of course,
or realised, or recognised, or even
known about. Think how the troubadours
found it a way of being more alone,
to make a rose fill with the sun and songs
of birds, an unreality we can't
renounce and keep our souls, as Hannah Arendt

wrote imagining those skeleton-
like figures bending to machines, or how
locked in the luxury of this freedom
we still consume our sugar walls, and now
reality itself, the TV show
(Big Brother was a cuddly name to choose)
that pays for all the unreal talks and news.

Ventriloquism, CCTV, voice-
over, scenarios, sets, scripted shots,
and what they must compete to do – our choice,
we judge – is to be us, is to be not
rejected, as if in a village court
from home, that holds you in its gossip-speak
and when I bend to kiss you, shifts your cheek

to watch the unreal houseguests being watched
as they turn real, are realised, are who
eats cornflakes, who annoys you, or you mock
or stand beside, that towel across the boobs,
that brush on lash, but can't be answered *you*
however straight they look into the lens
at us, we millions, till the close-up ends,

we stolen souls — and no it's all about
this *soul society*, you say, the issues
in its mystery play, the roles set out
for them to learn, to need, to turn into
and be, and fear this loss, this walking through
the exit, to applause no doubt after
such definition, close up as a lover's

every which way part by part of her
rehearsed in turn, the steel-tipped heel, the ankle,
calf, thigh, waist, breast, neck, lips, forehead, hair —
that could be Bertran's analytical
construction of a woman from the swirl
of that one's earlobe, the slim wrist of this,
the exiled gaze that rests so wide in his —

stolen souls: a superstition attributed to Africans and others by
explorers was that they feared the camera stole away their souls
Bertran's analytical construction: Ezra Pound in a note to his Na
Audiart, refers to Betran's song "wherein he... begs of each pre-
eminent lady of Langue d'Oc some train or some fair semblance...
to make... a borrowed lady or as the Italians translate it, 'Ina donna
ideale'."

as wide as Aquitaine, Arabia,
the Music Hall, my mother tongue, Mum who
cried through her Irving Berlin tunes with more
than wartime tenderness, the ragtime Jew
who God-blessed Uncle Sam with *yous* and *trues*
and *feeling blues* and blue notes in a scale
that once the slaves had made out of the wail

of Yankee army brass just with their breath,
and no-one except God to entertain,
no whistles and applause for them, not yet,
no Mr Interlocutor, no names
of coonbands on the bakelite, no fame,
no lights but candle lights that move towards
us now, God listening, for her, Comfort,

a horn to sing in grief for her, to cry
instead of her, for all of them: Kakka, Ephraim,
Mamma, Babba, always their stares inside
the walls, around the curves of roads that come
into your windscreen every day, and claim
themselves for sadness, helpless as they are,
as are your eyes turning to windscreen glass,

as is her voice still in the phone, Comfort's,
as close as in your skull – Comfort who's dead
because of what? Because this diabetes
God would heal for her there in her bed
at home, since she was His and had no dread
of *spiritual attack* which was the cause –
somewhere, far back inside somebody's eyes

fixed on the road, who couldn't cope and drove
his fifty miles to work in Zaria,
to get away from death, from her, from love
whatever that had been, and left her there,
bloated and bed-sored with mad-woman's hair,
(and Jo, his Shell Oil Secretary daughter
too scared of the death to come either).

He was a missionary man. He'd learnt,
about the ethics of devoted labour,
swept her house, went to the market, turned
his fifteen-year-old bride into a giver
of donations to those holy hangers
on of God who'd kneel with her and bid
the evil spirit keep away. It did.

At night you speak to her and call her *you*
as if she'll answer, or just smile or nod
or turn away, avoid your eyes, pooh-pooh
the very grievous foolishness of what
you're trying, with that toss-flick of her head
it's you imagining, that mime in which
it's she, it feels, who's your ventriloquist.

Your second mother and her nose and brow
exactly yours, your own flesh history,
look, outlined for a moment on the window
now, still here, still here, in mimicry
is it or camouflage, the way the spirits
stay with those who can remember them,
and whom they visit like this in a dream,

a caller sitting on your bed to chat
and joke, 'catch up', and be alive again,
because now you're her afterlife no matter
what she has deserved, or might have been,
whatever flesh she might have once belonged
to as it's *I*, and *you*, and *you* now only
through a form of words, a courtesy.

(There's Lara, forty, reading to her son,
and me a clown face on a see-through skull,
her hand about to turn the page, *and then...*
and in the skull the relics of those cells
by which a baby feels somebody else's
eye or limb or voice inside their own,
a proto love, a peaceable kingdom

in which the mathematics of a cello
string's translating all the tadpoles in
the pond, as once did Dad's piano notes,
along a line of melody, of ink
that goes on thinking what it's trying to think
but hasn't found, and can't, a scribbled draft
of something drafted as a draft for that.

And yet the paradox that it should matter
what'll happen to my daughter when
I'm just a syllable or so, if that,
of chatter sometimes on her lips, in them
perhaps, exiled perhaps, in that *and then*
that calls the tale to its own exile in
its sentences, where there's no mattering.)

The sense of exile, as the sense of home,
the prep school woods turning to Africa –
the somewhere else – then real, to Number Ten,
to markets, students, you, and you another
exile far off here, home as it were,
as an address the nurse holding her pen
and chart in Gynie asked for, then again,

and him an exile too, the blood-smeared one,
the tearful stranger whose hand knows it must
grip someone very tightly and hang on
and could be anyone, another lost
arrival who'll acclimatize, who's gazed
at and sees gazes in his gaze, and whom
the empty sound of *you* gets whispered to,

his syllable, this sign, this interference
getting in the tune as well, its hiss
its close, its taste, its warm, its soft, its scent,
its tickly hair, its red, its breath, its kiss,
that come back, that come back when his own lips
can mime the sound, yet when he says it, *you*,
it's he himself that he's referring to.

Your children are your exile too: they've never
built a cooking fire, or pounded, hoed,
wondered if those are soldiers' or armed robbers'
silhouettes, have no accent to go
back to and meet the voices of, and no
bend in the orange road's a different light,
longing for which gets worse when people die.

When they're grown up and when I'm dead, yes keep
that tryst you've got in you, and go, and settle
back, laugh with the women as you sweep
a compound, get work at a hospital –
a shudder-dripping fridge, no drugs, blunt needles –
you with *been-to* eyes, the green passport,
the red, the face of you each one distorts

with being neither, nowhere, to be shown
at barriers you've come to from your far
off ECWA school, that face filmed on the cabin
glass on bevelled sea, here on the sofa
watching TV where dead Henry Moore
says happiness to him's in this stone child
and mother waiting against empty cloud.

been-to: A Nigerian who has visited Europe.

(I keep on dreaming about children, one
who clasped me as I held him and he shook
and cried, no name or even face, just some
soul metaphor, myself, my son, his cheek
against my dreamer stubble once, as like –
as much – me as himself, and me the same,
and nameless too but for that given name.

I don't know what to make of the *unconscious*
any more, no more than imagery,
the middle-class pale lips a dream's supposed
to whisper omens in, solidify
into a sculpture that fills up the sky
with imitations of a tenderness
that needed so much granite to express.

What did he want? Shaping and shaping it?
The Kingdom of a kind. Like Jon's. I miss
him now, there in the rain among the prams
selling his sheaves of *Stand*, the crying kid
life long in him. Where have they come from, these
children? These children? Whom we have to turn
to poems, or to news, or dreams, or stone?)

Jon: Jon Silkin, poet, founder editor of *Stand*.

Go back? To Elli, then? Who's been your kin
and blood life long, Go back? Find something left
of Babba in the market cries of Sabon
Gari and the smell of rain in dust,
and pale green oranges, again, and rusted
corrugated roofs, the speech, the smile
of greeting as you raise a hand and call

it back, *Malam, my friend*, the vocative
as you've since learnt, containing *So you're still
alive*, or as Babba would say, *alive
again*, the way your kids are going to fill
the place of *I* you now look through the pupils
of as if it doesn't matter whose
it is, which self is self, which you is you.

And they'll go back, as foreigners, to gaze
at graves — Comfort's, Mamma's, Babba's, their kin
known more like ancestors, to be amazed
by shaking alleluias, crashing rain —
the house my spirit comes to still, again,
where it was happier than anywhere
and melts awhile into its gorgeous air.

Amina's come and there's her saddened marriage
in that long hug with the door still open,
and the kids waiting, as if they're stranger
in their own *parlour* and glance of garden
through a window, than they are, become,
here where the voices turn back into Hausa
asking – and I find that I remember

all the words I knew, though not enough
then either – who's now where, or dead? Some are,
like Bala Usman, that limp helpless sleeve
he guided with his other hand, remember,
from the crash – or the attempted murder,
Hauwa interjects, eyes hard and certain
where her mind is moving, has remained,

before all else, all since, her kids, this West,
that brings back Mimi's version of Faiz:
"Our lives have more to answer to," he says,
"than love," thinking about the whine of flies
after the bombers leave, some broken child
in rubble, some mother who bites her cuff
and looks at him – with nothing *else* than love.

Bala Usman (1945-2005): Nigerian historian, lecturer and
political activist
Mimi: Mimi Khalvati, *The Chine*, p 78

Oh lizard in the garden, you who swell
into a technicolor dream, into
The Worm sliding through softly clicking jewels
in the cave where brave Dreamself must go
and face you deafened by the roars of echoes
in his head, which echo in his veins
like tuning forks because he is a man,

subject to tone and pitch, and doesn't run,
because the virtues he must have require
that he come back again into the sun,
betray no PTSD, no nightmares
lying in wait as if the dragon's there
again, and whole, always, behind the gaze
of love he turns towards his lady's face

as yes it is, behind the words, beneath
the *character* being whispered in his ear
by that angel as unreal as the breath
it's whispering, nothing but words, and fear
of nothing else but words, the voice as near
as your voice in my phone, my head, you who
lack time and place for all this *I am you.*

Quaint is his supermodel's blue distain
for all who look on her, and on the fabric
of her elegance, on her unbidden
look back with the eyebrows and the trick
of nothing except strange out of a pic
he's gazing at imprisoned in his cell,
or hers, where she will ransom him, console,

convert him into her, as if that's who
he's always been, and he can come and come
out of himself through her, then, through and through,
still dark as *are* the walls of that stone womb
he's lifted from, running with thick red slime,
and her hand moving also in his head,
inside the moving nerves, her voice instead

of his to mean himself until he learns,
unlearns, and like me comes back to the lost
half-state Walcott (at Canterbury) termed
this state of metaphor: the black-faced ghost
of Bonaparte in Toussaint's tattered vest,
these songs, and these quaint tales of men who live
and die for love as is their privilege.

Toussaint: François Dominique Toussaint L'Ouverture (1743-1803),
Haitian anti-colonialist revolutionary.

The Black Stalin, the Black Napoleon –
and then I thought of smiling Joe Mbele,
1980, at last going home
to build the soviets of new Zimbabwe,
turning in his dusty drive for me
to snap him getting in the car, one hand
still lifted on my desk where he still stands

next to the cutting he's sent with a photo
of queues zigzagging out of the frame
and with the creases for the envelope
pressed in it, no letter, address, or name,
just biro capitals: THE BANKNOTES RAIN
DOWN LIKE CONFETTI, and I see the glisten
of the grin he hides his homeland in,

because he gave himself to that and not
just someone's eyes, *the individual*
he'd say making his face wrinkle about,
and on the internet I find the so-called
vets have knocked him down in some hotel,
same name, at least, and *who was elderly*
it says. Forgodsake, he was seventy!

Black Stalin: an imaginary needed dictator looked for by some
radical Nigerian intellectuals in the 1980s
Black Napoleon: a name sometimes given to François Dominique
Toussaint L'Ouverture.

Quaint as the shot silk starlings in the field,
the shine of grass, or as the sudden flush
of scent outside when our blue moonflower yields
itself and all the spreading petals push
just that one night a year, or as the bush
Yuri Zhivago saw and spoke her name
aloud – Lara! – so very far from home.

Quaint as the garden, smart of cut and edge
and measured daffodil where courtly bums
are floating smoothly by a hawthorn hedge
and out of it a blackbird darts and screams
in panic for her eggs left in that gloom
of twigs through which, from low down, once I'd spy
the dark clot of the nest against the sky,

the house that has a single shrinking wall,
the cave of plenty, sky or egg, or red
red cave of blood and out of it the wail
of being that the troubadour's not heard
because the singing of his jewelled birds,
because the dragon's scales, its breath, its claws
because this deafening stare of metaphor....

But you're the common human actual person,
who is here, is intimate, who could
have been somebody else, and for that reason
it's this hair, this neck, this chin, this foot,
this timbre in the voice, turn of the head –
in which my privilege consists, this *you*
to whom no matter who you are, love's due,

and when a stranger comes and I ask what
his name is, if he's hungry, where his village
is, his tribe, about his wife, about
his children, parents, I can feel the edge
of this cup in my hand, the way the patch
of light silvers your cheek as you too listen,
as you are, have become, different

in just being so much known, nothing to do
with romances except of course in this,
that everyone is always strange, being who
they are, if we, if I, can reach the muse
in them, in you, here with this trickster's gift
of sudden English flowers bubbling
with bees as soft as eyes, that cannot sting.

Because of love you are allowed to stay.
Because of love they stamp the visa forms.
Because of love, not theirs but ours, the *Daily
Mail, Daily Express, The Sun,* perform
their variations on the theme of home
and *them* and *not, won't, don't, might, could, should, shouldn't,
not-racist, asylum, immigrant,*

of *pole, sound bite, angle of camera shot,*
and *turbaned traitor* ranting about lies,
and deaths, and torture camps, for which we're not
responsible, not you, not I, not I,
my kids, my work, the objects that we buy,
no, even though we are so rich compared/
contrasted/relative to them, and scared –

of losing it, this inequality
we never asked for but which now we need,
we need, each one of us, watching TV,
driving to work, donating how much blood
we can afford, and which we owe, indeed
to them, like *love* itself for what it's worth:
the now more damned than ever of the Earth,

Damned: Les Damnés de la Terre, Franz Fanon

those who will make us safe, will save our lives
again as far away as once your Dad
turned soil now turning into dust, and rivers
shrink to shingle, then Islamabad,
Beijing, Mumbai, some mute AIDs-like attack
wide as a second flood and second rainbow
promising not too much carbon now,

and no strange-looking ones to spoil the style
made in the *Id's* own creativity
with sediment and dying plants, *to hell*
with all your welling up humanity,
as if this hasn't always been where we,
us here, have got our quiet houses from,
and you your time to wonder at the sun —

which ought to be enough, I'd want to say —
to eat, to love, to vote — to vote, to choose
and choose some other sense, more peaceably,
of who we are, of us, as us, and who's
the lizard in the skull, and now the hush
of sand towards the town, then road, then gate,
the path, the house to which we emigrate —

to which Rasheed has come on study leave
bringing you tastes of home: yaji, daddawa,
smoked fish from the market coiled in wreathes,
tail into mouth, that villagers from Hanwa
caught before contractors damned the river
so that when I walked along its bed
that time, the steep banks rose over my head.

For me, part *of* you *is* just that: the bush,
a dark tomato of a sun, the spokes
of big slow bikes along the paths, the hush
of kaftans as the farmers call their jokes
and greetings out across that sky, the hoes
hooked over backs, that wailing motorcade
as far off as a spirit from the dead.

The river gravel was exposed in tapered
wedges getting finer at the tips,
the steep bank showing roots that went down deeper
than the plant grew up, my dry footsteps
clinking the pebbles, no wind on my lips:
as if I'd been allowed to walk beneath
the water just this once and yet still breathe.

yaji, daddawa: condiments

What do I really know of that country
of yours, the hoped-for land in which I'd find –
oh, all these findings, these discoveries,
these looted treasures stashed away in mind
to be brought back and labelled with the sounds
of English words whose meanings I don't know –
an ignorance? That's what I have to show.

And how socratic is the wood-carved head
which I unwrap as if from waterproof
like Livingstone, and put next to our bed
still as a soul. I have to keep it, love.
Such contradiction has to be enough
although it's not, I know. It's like your known
voice intimately far off in a phone.

Like Rasheed's too, talking of Bessie Head
again from his MA analysis
out on the porch after he'd come and set
down rice bags in the kitchen, laughing, "Presents!" –
me not sure if they weren't something else
at first. But no, stones on the pages, dust
that gradually our voices didn't taste.

He used say I was his father, *babba*,
with that gratitude the students had.
Remember when we stayed once in Kaduna
and he came one morning with the wad
of naira for me, just to help a bit,
no thought I should repay, only a sense
of what is suitable (like bags of rice), –

the *if I have, or if you have, we give
of course* tradition that's now almost gone,
and he the chair of the committee of
new understanding between Christians
and Muslims, then the time that he saved Ben
who wouldn't give his source to the police
and R insisting that the rule was his,

the editor's, and *nothing to do either
with Allah or God*, and finally
the smiles at that, the slapping handshakes over
groundnuts being passed around, and me
being introduced as teacher come to see
if he's still working hard, and then the eyes
of the inspector full on mine, with joy,

naira: Nigerian currency

52

and I the student, then, except to him
that wasn't possible, but still the link
that Socrates had made, came back – between
the way we learn to love and learn to think,
so that an ordinary blackbird sings
like something that, alas, it's not, or else
as something that just stands for *now* and *is* –

his house, his compound, then the ostriches
he's lifting Lara on the fence to see
the way their big pale lids and eye lashes
blink upwards, and her question about why
an ostrich is a bird if it can't fly
and him explaining how the wings of all
birds started as just things for keeping cool

and look how wonderful *he* is, my shrieking
cock who thinks that he can order dawns
to break just by the lifting of a beak
and his wings still no more than little fans
to flap for all the gold magnificence
imagined cosmic love renews each day,
so intimate it is, and far away.

He brings news of the killings: so-called *tribe*
on so-called tribe, and all goes back to oil
and looters in high places, banks and bribes,
and dead fish floating in a petrol smell.
I thought of Comfort's daughter who's with Shell
so-called Nigeria who's bidding's done,
out in the bush somewhere, just before dawn,

then of their house in '96, the walls
around it with barbed wire along the tops,
your in-law's gun, the dead man's broken skull
your nephew Charles had seen with wet brain slopped
on dust. Then, '86 after they'd stopped
the quelling of the students on the campus
a thinning mist, the faintest sting of gas.

Still there, are they, yards from the office, bullet
pock marks in the wall with felt tip O's
around each one, the total counted? Protests,
speeches, loud hailers, then Kill and Go,
Farida shot still in her shower robe
as she went back along the balcony
towards her room. God, my inadequacy!

Kill and Go: armed mobile police

Rasheed was editor in chief. He knew
them face to face, of course, Ken Saro Wiwa
who was done because of Alli who
had nursed this grudge, Abacha who was murdered
by the CIA – call-girls, viagra,
poison, agent Coleman.... How sheltered
I am, this teacher, due so much respect.

My good pupil. I see him, at Heathrow:
the line of babban rigas for Abuja,
stacked up excess bags. Before he goes
he bends to give Tristan and Laraba
"something". He waves. He goes into Departures.
We turn back, slot in the carpark fee,
and search our well-known darkness for A3.

This is safe England where shysters like Blair
mix easy words and pictures, some, at least,
part true to tell us of a country far
away and strange with different customs, feast
days, and a wicked King whose wicked secrets
hide so deep down in the tale we haven't
found them yet. They keep us innocent.

babban rigas: traditional flowing Hausa robes

I gave him sterling to pass on to Joe
who runs the English office still, and eats
meat once a week these days and is supposed
to buy goats now that he's been made a chief
but can't afford to. Swivelling on his seat
he'd swivel back with any doc I wanted
from that filing system in his head.

I studied it, this Africa, its use
of English in its poetry, Ikebe
Super, Pidgin. I wrote to dispute
the thesis put forward by Ngugi
wa Thiong'o when he seems to say
that English words plug Africans with English
thoughts, surely quite unmaterialist...

I did a little bit. Got Awam in,
and Jenks, and Mbulelo, kept the VC's
buddies out, began a mag, got Pidgin
on the syllabus. Though none of this
would outlast Maigida's return to be
true head again, and send out the Department
car to Sabo to collect his rents.

Ikebe super: literally 'super bum', popular tabloid magazine

In '98, when we came back, there's Joe
grinning and pointing at the bucket on
the floor to catch the drips. Down south Okpewho,
Soyinka, Achebe, Biodun,
'Molara, Femi, Kole, they've all gone
where they can work: The States, South Africa,
UK. Our HOD's now bloody Emma!

Flight of the scholars. No more annual
conferences held in Ibadan now
nor Calabar where you came once when still
on NYS, and we walked with Okello
to the jetty and that clanking grew
into a blurry shadow on the mist
that for a moment was the Heart of Darkness

steamer on the Penguin book (a row
of them along the shelf behind Joe's head):
the river and the blur of primal Congo
where the white man trekked to meet his id,
Achebe wrote, Joe's townsman, whom I met
once in that room, Joe overawed, I'm thinking
as he smiles, smiles still and those drips plink.

NYS: National Youth Service, done – in an area of the country
they don't come from – by all students after graduation
Okello: Okello Oculi, the Ugandan poet, novelist and political scientist
Achebe: Chinua Achebe, Nigerian novelist, author of *Things Fall Apart*

I learnt, teaching my language, that it's *differen-*
differen here, and that the words I *use*
to use don't mean the same *again*, that phonemes
captured by the native speaker fuse
with market stalls and flies and how in those,
dear *talkative*, dear *gister*, still the sound
of *no hear*, means *I do not understand.*

And coming home I thought that I'd revert
to standard, not hear in *I think, I hope*,
but no: I still say *sorry* if you're hurt,
and don't mean I'm to blame. I still say *soup*
for stew, and sometimes call a glass a cup,
for all the words in your idiolect,
I still get wrong, no hear, or no detect.

And every word I say might be untrue
since that's how language works, not like a flip
I might reset, repair, replace, re-fuse,
but what, in every syllable that lips
have ever breathed, it is, in every hiss
of yes, and every semi-vowel of love
for which, of course, no words are words enough.

differen-differen: Nigerian non-standard English: 'completely different,
to be contrasted'
use to use: Nigerian non-stardard English: 'usually use'
again: Nigerian non-standard English: 'still'
gister: one who 'gists,' chats to pass the time
no hear (Hausa): 'ji' means 'sense', including 'hear', but also 'understand'

I'm reading about Certainty the odd
senses the word *know* can take on, the way
I know you're on the sofa there, but not
because I gaze more closely at your eyes
or lips or plaits: just the insanity
of doubting it, and then I think of tales
of men's eyes gazing from their pectorals....

And this to do with stern Miss Browne, and *West*
chalked on the blackboard with a compass arrow
pointing at the Shrewsbury Arms, and East
towards the conker tree, to do with Andrew
Philpot when she asks him, "Come on now,
Andrew, a noun of place?" – and with her anger
when he says again: "There, in that corner!"

Nothing more certain than my gumboots there,
or that the bell would go, Mum be at home,
the fields, the garden fence, sun on the car –
although we left and all that proof is gone,
as that of prep school has, now Number Ten.
What's certain's certain just in retrospect?
And when I die which boxes will you check?

Certainty: Ludwig Wittgenstein, *On Certainty.*

And you're not certain, are you? All this love,
this love, all this sincere, all this declare,
admit, confess, these syllables, these puffs
of breath still warm that break across your hair
your cheek, these speech balloons, this inner air
whose certainty can only be incurred?
I say I love you but it's only words.

What difference can words make, and English words
at that, and *full of grammah*, that Bature
tok whose stress and tune you never heard
at school, and don't quite fit reality,
not even now, not even here, where they,
like yours, contain another kind of earth.
I say I love you but it's only words.

As if the rocks and loam create a tongue,
as though the meaning were geography,
another kind of rain, another sun.
But that's only a metaphor, the way
that love alas prompts us so readily
to plant the desert full of magic herbs.
I say I love you but it's only words.

full of grammah: using sophisticated standard English

Home as the setting, as the narrative,
the starting point, the past? The soul, maybe,
before the longing came? The tale you live
as it comes back to you or as somebody
tells it, re-tells it, as you tell me?
A dawa fence? A swaying scarlet bird?
I say I love you, but it's only words.

The bullfrog hanging downward by its eyes
from surface tension on a village pond,
a moonlight sharp enough to draw the lines
of shadow between furrows – and so on,
so I imagine, as I've always done,
exploring as the Whiteman always would.
I say I love you but it's only words.

The Reith Lectures are on the theme of trust,
without which, as I read, I realise,
nothing coheres at all, and that's not just:
Have I spoken with truth to you? Did I
mean what I said? Or what I meant to try
to say or what you thought I had inferred?
I say I love you but it's only words.

Dawa: maize, stalks used for fencing
Reith Lectures: *A Question of Trust* by Onora O'Neil

61

I touch you. I imagine you. I change
you into words, my cells, my chemicals,
my sparks, my dancing spine. I make you strange.
I conjure you from common syllables,
from Kano market, Billingsgate, Arrivals.
I wait holding your biro name on cardboard.
I say I love you but it's only words.

The orphan you still are must justify,
must justify, must not (the phrase is just)
be found wanting, can't help it, nor can I,
that loss in you that drives out every trust,
and trust in doubt as well, and doubt as love
itself that touches you since you're a nurse.
I say I love you but it's only words.

I'll be your malam and bring magani.
I'll mix up something that'll staunch your fear
of needing me, some *mai gashin baki*.
I'll squeeze the droplets gently in your ears
until your eyes are bright, and onion tears
will seem to stand in them, but nothing worse.
I say I love you but it's only words.

malam (Hausa): traditional healer
Magani: medicine in the sense of traditional remedy
Mai gashin baki: literally, the one with the moustache, name of
patent medicine for all ailments. The label has a picture of a
white man with a moustache like Lugard's.

The glossy pages slosh across and come
to it, the human heart, the ventricles,
a section of the pericardium
or outer wall, and then the visceral,
the veins and valves, the systole diastole
of human metre with a sound like *lub*
and *dub*, or as if through a wall, like *love*.

Safe on the page with little arrows, captions,
insets, it's not like the Holby City
shots of that thing jumping in the surgeon's
reddened plastic gloves, so carefully
squared off with cloth, or electronically
monitored, suspended still as death
on by-pass where no pain or feeling's left.

Look down then, nurse, and set your ECG,
place the electrodes, switch on. All your hard
homework will come in now. Examine me.
Note what you see there, or what you've inferred
from that pen with no hand filling my card
with shaky peaks and troughs of lub and dub
that I can't hide, or alter, or make up.

Or stop, or start, or claim as mine, because
all that thing like a big ripe dark red mango
needs to do is stop. This drum-beat causes
me to stay alive yet all I know
about it comes from text books, now from you.
Pulse rate, shortness of breath, pain in the chest,
transferred like metaphor to somewhere else.

Or someone else, or breath, a baby's scream
for anyone at all – it doesn't matter
who she is so long as she'll just come,
from anywhere, and have life drawn from her,
and it be taken, all that lizard horror
from inside. She's got to. He exists,
a child, is there, no matter who he is.

It's not just *Roman de la Rose* then, this
old arrow head stuck in the heart that threatens
life itself, or those traces, at least
of when it might have and life did depend
on love, or something like. This eloquence,
lady, replaces such unmanly screams
with boxer shorts and wine, or so it seems.

And in the cooking fire, three blackened stones
set on the ground, and in the tinder sticks,
and in the logs, known without being known:
an ethics as unseen as common, *this*
next, *this* now, then the way the paper disk
you replace on my windscreen makes dates
dissolve and new ones fade up in their place.

Not quite to do with words for all the lips
and tongues of them that come and come and cry
with massive momentary joy and hips
melting like chocolate: to do not quite
with not-quite words, but the abstractions pride
and truth, your father's words not quite to do
with words, or so you say, love me or no.

Naïve, of course, and me no less naïve
to think that actions have no meanings *but*
in their description, which must be described,
which is an action too, or try to put
my case sentiment*al*, holding your foot
in both my hands, with slow words about who
I am, as if to make the words more true.

How hard it is to get down to this thought
that who we are's just webs of words and nerves
the gods of history and chance have caught
us in, not *I* at all, more like the urge
an actor has to lose himself and merge
into another self that has no self
except in being imagined someone else.

Dear Gizo-gizo, trickster spirit, friend,
lithe ageless optimist, you who'll give God
a run, still, for his money, in the end
the answers, too, are pranks, aren't they? And Sod
himself, the lawyer, he it is who prods
us gently in the ribs, and tries to smile:
You had no substance, man, all that was style,

and took it from the time, the place, the compound
wall, the washing line, the well, some blue
white ash over some cooking stones, a sound
of pounding, of cicadas. *Part of you,*
he says, *each one of these, that make up who
you are.* And who is that? And who is he,
to know so much of grass and stones and clay?

Gizo-gizo (Hausa): spider, trickster figure in folk fables

And *you*? A pointing word for who is there,
or was. It means not *he* or *she*, not *it*,
not *I,* nor *I* dissolving in a stare,
or made an actor's part, and limited
by that, or that last person to be greeted
who's not you at all yet still the one
you talk to as yourself, that everyman

who has accompanied you all this way
but must stop here, must raise a hand – to *you*,
is that? And who else is there? Well, maybe
those other representatives shot through
with *I* and *am*, those empathisers who
have nothing else, each one a candidate,
each one a soul, whose empathy is that,

who says, *I'll go with you, I'll go at least*
as far as makes no difference, old chap,
dear boy, now that there's nothing else to trust
except the child in you, and who is that?
a photo ghost: tuckbox and prep school cap,
the train, the whistle that goes on and on
until they switch it off and note the time.

And here's a soul? Pure light. Whose back is turned.
Whose plaits are bunched up with a clip. A gold
earring, a glasses' frame, a cheek outlined
against a cabinet of pale brown panelled
wood. No eyes, no face, to tell how old
the subject is. We'd have to wait until
she turns to face us, as she never will.

Except it seems to me you were about
to turn, had felt my lens on you, had paused
for it to click, the flash to shiver out,
the moment go, not wanting to be caught
full on, full in the face, or so I thought
if I recall it, fixed like this, the moment,
as it was, as I imagine it

except that this is all just empathy,
not yours, but mine, the mirrors in the slop
and forks and sparks of brain, my *pulmonary
variations*, on the theme of lub
and dub whose comic strip balloons come up
and stir the air towards you from my mouth.
Already they're half ink as they reach out.

All minstrelsy as well: the crumply tights,
the window lit up in the stone, the lute
to make the changes on and tune a sigh
to fret and interval, and make a *you*
out of the *you* vibrating in the gut
and throat and fingertips – which all connive
to sound as simple as a blackbirds' cry

just when the blue-black comes into the sky
above the front door where he waves the tinking
trafficators off, holding the coffee
still hot in his fist, something she thinks
that there's no need to do at all, something
to do with just that need, some prep school boy's
drilled reassurance in brave-eyed goodbyes,

or shape a gesture in the air that's still
a shape for loneliness, the troubadour
in him, that has to find the outer style
and out of that devise his metaphor
of who she is, and what he's singing for,
that she'll hear in his voice, perhaps, or won't
perhaps, or he will for her if she can't.

Or else, instead, just drive her into work:
sharing the lady with the lollypop
and melting butter coat, kids at the kerb,
the lights on early in the paper shop,
the wheeling town and ocean from the top
of Portsdown Hill, and then the hospital,
the car slamming, her quick look back and smile.

Such small goodbyes and goings out of sight,
like Tristan's hand lifting beyond the hedge
as he runs off, return sometimes at night
as I look back towards the shelves and fridge
from out there on the lawn beyond the grid
of windows shadowing the grass, alone,
as timeless as time is, homeless as home,

and just this sense of *here* itself is where
love doesn't come, for all that opiate
the village malam gave you to prepare
and sprinkle secretly onto my plate
of acha in Kagoma that time way
back when the trickster spirits nodded yes,
and without knowing what it was, I ate.

acha: a pottage whose name is taken from its main ingredient,
the grain 'acha'.

And no words words enough, or pictures. Scribble's
maybe closer to the helpless eyes
and stammerings, since it's not legible
and reaches for some limit speech denies
us with its own, towards a paradise:
red finches, oranges, pools, glistening carp
through ripples like the shaking of a harp,

a voice, changing the boughs to metaphors
of its own sound, and claiming that is love.
Or is it fear – that boy's face in the grass
as Heinkel's mythic fighter tipped to dive
towards him in the dream, and that black glove
poised just above the button as it came
and never came, again and yet again?

Or this garden. The bike left out, the pond
I dug and lined with plastic for the kids
where tadpoles coil and wriggle in a brown
they breathe a while among the waterweeds,
and are and aren't themselves, frogs no-one sees
although sometimes, too late, that splash behind
us makes us stop and try to catch the sound.

Heinkel's mythic fighter: the so-called Heinkel 113 fighter in World
War Two. In propaganda which the RAF swallowed it was a super
machine, but in reality not a new plane but the Heinkel 100
renamed, although in fact with better performance than the
famous Messerchmitt 109, which was chosen by Hitler for produc-
tion. The He 113 never saw action though 'kills' were recorded by
RAF pilots and it appeared in recognition manuals such as a small
boy might read and be impressed by.

Or else that other fear – or they're the same,
are they? – the dream plane falling and the lizard
listening mute for ever, sprawled against
the classroom wall, although its orange inner
mouth can roar so wide that in the terror
where it finds us we also are deaf,
no cry, no word, no gesture, nothing left

beyond the fight and flight bit that still comes
without a shape the way film music seeps
out of the leaves, or as the hillside thuds
with beats the brain had jammed, or as the beach
exhales breath after sleeping breath, still keeps
its camouflage of volume-turned-down flowers
waiting on this mantelpiece of ours,

or as that time the rainbow lizard darted
fast as thought out of the sun to kill
my spinning coin, but no, a lips-apart
clunk in the gums, a pause, and then a spilt
out tinkle on the concrete, his brain still
tricked by the mimicry of synapse time
in that ten-kobo flickering, like rhyme

or empathy things have with things, which as
it were, nobody thinks, the hiss of wasps
inside the mango turning into gas,
into the wind through trees now backs and tops
of shadowed chairs, as once the bullfrogs' grop
and grarp was *what a laugh*, and now the printer's
lisping whispers: *kith her, kith her, kith her*

as I bend across your sleep and switch
the lamp off and then see his indigo
and orange scales and claws sprawling to grip
on nothing, mirror nothing, there, below
all right and left, all I and you, zero
and one, evil and good, nature and law,
or sound or syllable or word or clause

by which the breath and lungs can legislate
in speech's own democracy, and where,
also, it's me entangled in the fate
of them, these lizard ganglia down here,
a while, if *me* makes sense, this puppeteer
piping of love you can't quite credit, or
quite want, or listen to, or listen for,

(I thought of Jaraba, of Jaraba
my cockerel, he who'd tilt and flick his profile
so quick there's a smear of coloured air
and then just swinging jowls like testicles –
until God jerks his head back, and God pulls
his beak apart and shuts his eyes and lifts
his neck until his claws strain on their tips

for that great klaxoning that he can't help,
bright generalissimo who doesn't see
the joke because the trees are flat and deaf
and all the edges all around the sky
are yellow with the noise that has no pride
or shame left but a mime still echoing
its crackly everywhere and everything.

Of Jaraba, whose lust was just for lust,
and that a kind of love itself, that cries
with splitting beak still from my compound dust
and tells the sun once more when it should rise,
my hero who has wings that cannot fly,
my messenger who's message is the same
again and yet and again and yet again.)

Jaraba (Hausa): (i) overpowering desire, (ii) misfortune, accident

except of course you do, if I can find
my broken English self in this Onitsha
How to Play Love chapbooking of mine,
my *Dearest Heavenly Comfort* kosher
from the *Rules of Love*, its Eleanor
of Aquitaine whose market stall is set
with love's new agony and etiquette

to marry style and sense well-well in this
its own English – as unearthly as Lara's
cello lifting into apple trees,
until the apples fill with it, the stars
in harmony as well, along the bars
she counts through as she draws the bow across
those strings whose meaning lies in artifice,

in us, in all of us, in you, the bright
red crater of you from which she is lifted
slithery and shouting with the might
of all her life into my hands, as if
the tears of things were even so a triumph
running down the cheeks of that unknowing
face of love made in their crumpling.

Onitsha chapbooks/pamphlets: popular literature from the town of
Onitsha in Eastern Nigeria, with stories and articles about western
style 'romance' and love etiquette, in non-standard English. The
'play' love vocabulary love suggests the origins of courtly love as, at
first, a sophisticated 'game'.

I know – and then forget – it doesn't mean
you haven't heard me if your gaze is not
on mine, or then say nothing, or just turn
into the kitchen, and the sound of crocks,
the radio, your singing – all these acts
on acts along a line of fingertips
on things, the window light shining your lips –

make matter grammar, like your father's own
unspokenness out of his photograph
above the fire, his soft white turban on,
the lips, more Elli's, pushed into a half
just slightly crooked smile, the arcs
of grin-lines from his nose wings to his chin,
as if the spirit still looks out of him

at us – gentle policeman, court-clerk, farmer,
Christian, he with his truth and pride,
whose words have stayed in you, and whom you answer
also without looking, as if sometimes
his face, also, in faint scraperboard lines
waits in the darkness, no need now to speak,
nor you, all his advice long since complete.

You were eleven when he died, and then
all that was left were hours through the days
and mundane things to see his being in
however changed, or in somebody's gaze
out of a school textbook or in the names
on maps, in me sometimes in this land where
he's not, like love, and love like light through air,

has no appearance but the surfaces
of other things, or so it seems, then only
if reflected in the splitting lenses
of our everyday that makes them, maybe
visible, but still now what you see,
as in the different meanings that a deed,
perhaps an act of love, might have, and hide.

His son-in-law has never built a fire
of logs and little boulders, never blown
the tinder with pursed lips until it flares,
or born pots on his head, or swung a hoe,
or broken toe-nails against stones – or known
the silent actions and the diligence
that made it up: love's insignificance.

Acknowledgements

Parts of this poem, some in slightly different forms, have appeared in the following magazines to whose editors acknowledgement is due: *Acumen, Ambit, Agenda, Kunapipi, Poetry London, Poetry Review, Poetry Wales, Pratik, Stand, Wasafiri.*

I am very grateful indeed to the Society of Authors for generous financial help.

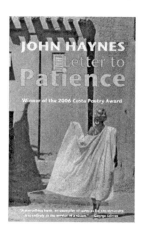

Winner of the 2006 Costa Poetry Award

Set in Patience' Parlour, a small mud-walled bar in northern Nigeria, at a time of political unrest, *Letter to Patience* is a vividly atmospheric book-length poem divided into cantos. The letter writer is in Britain, where he has returned with his Nigerian wife and children to nurse his dying father. He writes to Patience, the bar's owner, who once lectured in politics but who gave up due to junta pressures. The writer's thoughts range from his childhood to the present: from African myths to personal histories, from political violence to its tragi-comic consequences. The poem is not only a biography, or an essay on post-colonialism, it is an epic portrayal of a beautiful and troubled country and of one man's search for meaning in difficult times.

"Our unanimous choice... a clear winner." – Elaine Feinstein reporting the judges' verdict for the 2006 Costa Poetry Award

"...hums with energy, all manner of ideas and references jostling at the line breaks." – John Greening, *TLS*

"...human, tangible, capable of deep feeling, understanding, interpretation and intellectual wonder at the same time."
– George Szirtes, *Poetry Review*

"As a poet of autobiographical realism on a grand scale, Haynes is the equal of Muldoon, Heaney and Hill, while his philosophical self-effacement is all his own." – Jeremy Noel-Tod, *Guardian*